Words	**Jerry Holkins**
Illustrations	**Mike Krahulik**
Layout	**Dabe Alan**
Edits	**Kristin Lindsay**

LEXCALIBUR - USEFUL POETRY FOR ADVENTURERS ABOVE AND BELOW THE WORLD

© 2017, Penny Arcade Inc.
Lexcalibur and the PA Logo are trademarks of Penny Arcade Inc.

All rights reserved. No part of this book may be used or reproduced in any manner whatsoever without written permission except in the case of brief quotations embodied in critical articles and reviews. For more information contact info@penny-arcade.com or feel free to reach out to @cwgabiel & @tychobrahe on that bird tho.

First Printing: November 2017. Printed in China.

ISBN: 978-0-9971619-1-5

www.penny-arcade.com

For my enemies, who have made me wise

9	The Eyes Have It	29	Grummt
10	Good Advice About Bad Advice	31	House Darkmagic
11	Lesser Known Werebeasts	32	Acquisitions Incorporated
12	Surprise	33	One Man's Treasure
14	The Riddle of Black Bridge	35	Lorval's Larder
15	Sword of My Fathers	36	Irony Lesson
16	The Last of the Red Seekers	38	Girl-at-Arms
17	Elves of the Dolorus Valley	40	The Contents of Vault 23-B-Jackdaw
19	Vizier	40	The Contents of Vault Ex-X-Oriole
20	Doomblade	41	The Gnomish Bank of Philindem
21	The Inn at Frosthome	43	Guardian's Lullaby
23	Packing for the Deeper Realms	44	Weapons and Their Kin
24	Kaliak Siir Tells It Like It Is	44	Sunbeam, Son or Daughter
26	Too Many Dragons	45	On Villainy
28	The Swordhouse	46	Three Swords

The Eyes Have It

Don't jump to conclusions
Because I'm an eyeball
That floats through the hallways
And glistens with drool.
Technically, yes:
My hair is more eyeballs.
But ask any monster!
They'll tell you I'm cool.

Good Advice About Bad Advice

Some books may be comfortably
Judged by their covers.
Some people who wander
Can't find their way home.
Some caves are just mouths
Where strange birds may hover.
Some brothers are brigands,
Some sisters are gnomes.

Lesser Known Werebeasts

Everyone's talking about silly old werewolves,
Howlin' old werewolves, nobody cares.
There's buckets of were-things that you never heard of.
Lurking in darkness, scheming in lairs.

But where are the weres no one's ever heard of?
Friends, there are weres we know only a third of.

Please spare some pity for gentle were-kitties,
Sleeping all fuzzy in big plate mail boots.
And do take a moment for all the were-rodents
The were-kitties chase 'til the big were-owl hoots.

It's late in the were-swamp, were-toads are leaping.
Do try and be quiet! The were-beds are sleeping.

Surprise

What could be in there?
Mystical helms?
With jewels and strange letters
From faraway realms?
Or maybe a cape
With silvery stitching,
To shield me from magic
When witches are witching.
Could be a necklace,
With gold and gems strung;
But, no! It's just teeth.
Well, teeth and a tongue.

The Riddle of Black Bridge

There's letters underneath the bridge,
But nobody can read them.
Peter said his father said
That someday we may need them.

When our dads were young, I'm told
The words down there were clearer.
They burned with noble purpose
When the magic winds were nearer.

When the giants came, we looked
Beneath the sooty stone:
The words that had been written there
Were dull, and barely shone.

There's letters underneath the bridge,
But nobody can read them.
And since no one can read them,
well,
nobody can heed them.

Sword of My Fathers

The blade, well, it's nothing to look at.
And this hilt has seen better days.
The crossguard is dented from guarding
The tang and the leather part ways.

The pommel fell off in the forest,
I'll have to find it, or try.
But the scabbard, it says in clear letters
"With you, as ever, am I."

The Last of the Red Seekers

Karak the Wizard,
collector of gizzards,
Froze to death when he got himself lost in a blizzard.
Sir Harold the Knight,
Died of a fright,
Was raised from the dead, died again the same night.
Minna the Thief, please pardon my grief,
Disagreed sharply with very rare beef.
I'm the cleric, but then
I got changed to a hen.
Lucky for me, I can still hold a pen.

Elves of the Dolorus Valley

Elves of Morning, you should know,
do not like Elves of Evening.
If Evening Elves start coming 'round,
Then Morning Elves are leaving.

Double Elves are twice as tall,
and Sapling Elves are little.
River Elves are always running;
Peanut Elves are brittle.

Tender Elves are somewhat firm,
ask their sons and daughters.
Balmy Elves are somewhat hot,
but prob'ly could be hotter.

Feather Elves aren't Elves at all!
They're birds with little tufts.
They look sort of like an Elf,
and maybe that's enough.

Vizier

Viziers are so utterly evil.
A vizier is never a friend.
He takes no vacation
From his grim vocation.
So don't have a vizier.
The end

Doomblade

Some blades have a skull or two
Or three smalls skulls, at most.
But there's a sword tucked in this hoard
With ten skulls. And a ghost.

It couldn't be more spooky -
You have to see this thing.
You pull it from a long, thin skull,
And hold a skull to swing.
It's not the most convenient;
It's hard to use on prey.
But if you ever take it out,
Your foes all run away.

The Inn at Frosthome

There's a cat named Bildadr
With milk in a saucer
And reading a book
With her whiskers awry.
She is no one's cat,
Which means she's her own.
She is granted a nook
And a light to read by.

There's a sword on the mantle
That once was a weapon,
And now is a memory:
Hilt
And a flame.
Everyone says it's a sword
That they know of,
But they don't remember
A word of its name.

There is an inn
In the wood they call Frosthome,
So cold it is,
And no stranger to storm.
But if you can find it–
The sword– it stands ready,
The cat, she is reading;
The beds are all warm.

Packing for the Deeper Realms

Pack all your torches, and then,
Having packed them,
Get all your axes, wherever you've racked them.

Polish your swords up. Grind out the nicks.
A dungeon is no place
For waving sharp sticks.

But.

You may as well pack one,
In case all your swords
And axes get mangled by Mangling Wards.

Pack one sack for gemstones,
A helm for your face,
then pack two more torches.
You know.
Just in case.

Kaliak Siir Tells It Like It Is

I'll give you my opinion,
As a dragon of renown:
If you see a human, well,
You've got to gulp one down.

An elf is much too stringy,
And a werewolf has those claws.
If you see a human, though,
Just stuff one in your jaws.

Dwarves aren't much for eating.
You've got to eat a bunch.
But if you're near a human town,
Do stop on by for lunch.

Avoid the ones with armor on;
Stay clear of those with bows.
But humans are delicious, friend!
And trust me:
I would know.

Too Many Dragons

Some people say that one dragon's too many.

26

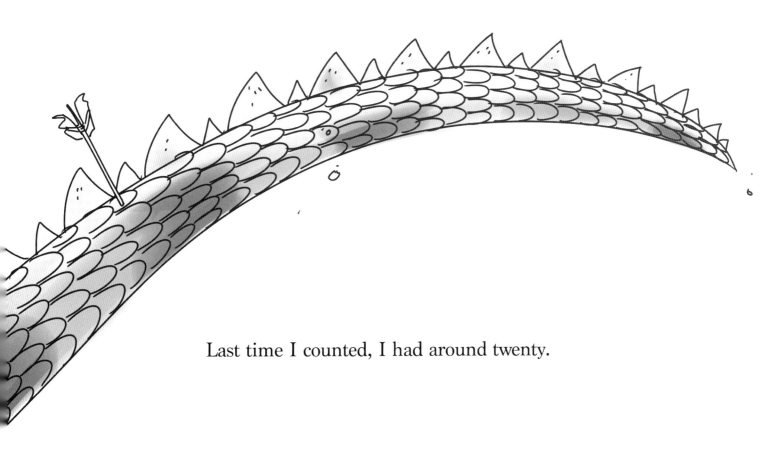

Last time I counted, I had around twenty.

The Swordhouse

There is no shortage
Of breathless reportage
On blades that draw dizzying
Arcs in the air.

Town squares all murmur
With barely-held fervor
About some long battle
Of some men
Somewhere.

Fewer are stories
Which recount the glories
Of those who could have drawn a sword
But did not;

If only they blabbered
On the noble scabbard
The way they do swords, well,
It might help a lot.

Grummt

There is a green leaf troll,
Leaf troll, leaf troll,
There is a green leaf troll
Green as a leaf.

There is a green leaf troll,
Leaf troll, leaf troll,
Who likes a little sweet roll
And a slice of beef.

House Darkmagic

Darkmagic wizards, they hold no truck
With demons or devils, but still, the name stuck.

Darkmagic warlocks are gentle and sweet;
They're never found prowling for children to eat.

Darkmagic sorcerers, to the last wand
Of darkness are not especially fond.

There's maybe one Darkmagic who bears the name
Who might be considered somewhat less than tame.
He hasn't been seen for years; wipe your brow.

`There's no reason to think that he'd show up just now.

Acquisitions Incorporated

If you've lost a something,
And now you can't find it,
Makes sense to call gents
To re-find who've refined it.

One thin one, one short one,
One regular sized;
And they only bill
When they've found what you prized.

No ghost too ghastly,
No lion too maned,
No giant too vasty,
No mind-beast too brained.

If you happen to find
What you sent them to find,
Do send them a note
That says "never mind."

One Man's Treasure

If you're going in search of
Some treasure divine,
Listen to me.
I can save you some time.

The Guardian Statues
Take Spring and Fall off.
If you want 'em in Autumn,
They're likely to scoff.

The Crown of Great Sorrow
Is kind of a bummer.
The Gold Baths of Grida's
In need of a plumber.

The Many-Shoe Stockings
Can only make clogs.
The Wolf-Master Circlet's
Allergic to dogs.

The Invincible Tunic
Is fine, I suppose,
If you like wearing
Three hundred pound clothes.

Lorval's Larder

If you have tired of commonplace food;
If you don't want to eat, but don't want to seem rude;
If you slaver for flavors that aren't so subdued,
Then stop by Lorval's Larder.

Her Larder, it trundles around on a cart,
That's halfway together and halfway apart,
And when you approach, she might wake with a start;
And say "Welcome to Lorval's Larder."

She has jars of something, and candied things too,
One hundred colors of cheese, not just bleu;
Red wyvern's eggs in a savory roux,
Boxes of foxes (as pets, not to chew),
Savory nuts (good in salad, or stew).
And she's sure to run out soon, so do join the queue,
To load up at Lorval's Larder.

Irony Lesson

I got a ring, and it makes me invisible.

No one can see me! A marvelous thing!

As I suggested, your eyes have been bested.

Completely invisible.

Except for the ring.

37

Girl-at-Arms

She can play at princess,
If that's what she wants to do.
Might not be my first choice,
But it isn't mine to choose.

She can be a wizard
If she finds a wand she likes.
She can be a ranger
If she feels like taking hikes.

She can be a roguish one,
'Twas always good at hiding.
She could be a Girl-at-Arms;
Such is her skill at riding.

She might be a thing for which
No one has made a name;
She may chart a course for those
Who want to do the same;

She might have left the world behind,
To dwell in velvet Space,
But I'll keep a plate for her
At dinner just in case.

The Contents of Vault 23-B-Jackdaw

One vial spring water: source is unknown.
One handful dirt (in which coins had been sown,
Like seeds, one supposes) plus one wind-up man
Who weeps in his hands like a drip in the sands

Of a desert. That is, it serves no good purpose.
One polished dream-lens, ready for purchase.

The Contents of Vault Ex-X-Oriole

Three large brown gloves, all alike for some reason;
One doll which laughs at the change of the season.
One clever fish with a rod to catch men,
One man on the line, saying "Never again!"

He'll be caught tomorrow, his oath to misspend;
The line is a thread with a coin at the end.

The Gnomish Bank of Philindem

Gnomes are not the tallest folk,
Nor are they the shortest;
But that is neither here nor there:
Their vaults are like a fortress.

They can, and do, store valuables
For those who know the system:
Deposit Holes are everywhere.
It's possible you missed them.

Opening a breadbox,
And then a second time,
Or give a stump a quarter turn,
And wait to hear the chime.

Their vaults are named for winged things
For few gnomes ever see them,
They churn there in the torchlit dark
And dream one day to be them.

Guardian's Lullaby

I've taught kings their manners, child,
Wrangled the thanes.
I've sheathed all the bitter blades
West of the Crane.
I beg of you, child,
As the wheat begs the rain,
to sleep.

I've parleyed with centaurs, child,
Knelt at the feet
Of leaf-laden forest kings
Thick with deceit.
I beg of you, child,
while the rain falls in sheets,
to sleep.

From the tooth of that mountain, child,
All of the way
To the reefs that lie, reaching
'round Tourmaline Bay
Children are doing
what their parents say:
to sleep!

My horses are weary, child,
I'm weary, too,
From making this world
a place worthy of you.
What is your bidding, child?
What must I do
to sleep?

Weapons and Their Kin

Everyone knows now
That swords live in Families,
That daggers have Covens,
And axes, their Clans;

That spears have a Sister,
That shields have a Brother,
That wands have another wand
That they can't stand;

That bows dwell in Clutches,
And hammers in Halls,
And lances,
Poor lances,
Have no friends at all.

Sunbeam, Son or Daughter

If you are born a son to me,
Sunbeam will be your name,
And if a daughter you shall be,
I'll call you just the same;

For from the top of parapets,
And from the mouth of coronets,
Baronetess, or Baronet,
It ever was your name.

On Villainy

There's some who is willin'
To win as a villain.
And child, you may as well let 'em.

'Cause sooner or later,
Their friends will turn traitor,
And some other villain will get 'em.

Three Swords

Three swords hanging from a tree
And none is like the other.
The tree was planted years ago
The seed was from my mother.

Heavy are they on the bough,
For they are growing, too;
They grow down, and I grow up,
And one day I will choose.

One day I'll be tall enough
To pick one, and leave two,
Or maybe it is choosing me,
And I just never knew.